WHEN THE CROSS
BECAME A SWORD

The Origin & Consequences
of Replacement Theology

MERRILL BOLENDER

WHEN THE CROSS BECAME A SWORD

Third Edition

Unless otherwise identified, Scripture quotations are from the New King James Version. Copyright © 1982 by Thomas Nelson, Inc. All emphasis in biblical quotations is the author's.

Cover design: Zyrek Castelino

Printed in the United Kingdom
For Worldwide Distribution.

Printed and bound by
CPI (UK) Ltd, Croydon, CR0 4YY

ISBN 978-0-9569448-4-9

Published and distributed by

Merrill Bolender—Psalm 71:18
P.O. Box 34478
Indianapolis, Indiana
46234-0478

mb.psalm.71.18@gmail.com

Acknowledgments

*"If I have seen further than others,
it is because I was standing on the shoulders of giants."*
ISAAC NEWTON

It is not possible to write a book such as this without borrowing extensively from other historian's studies.

I would like to express my appreciation to the many scholars whose work I have drawn from in the production of this work. To name a few, I would like to mention men like Derek Prince, Lance Lambert, Dr. Michael Brown, David Paulson, Fred Wright, Dr. John D. Garr, Erwin W. Lutzer, Robert Stearns, Chuck Cohen, Dr. Richard Booker, David Stern, Dr. Marvin Wilson, Peter Tsukahira and many others.

I don't lay claim to this material as it is more of a compilation of the work of many teachers and writers. I've collected material over the years from which I have gleaned to write this book. I've attempted to give credit to others where needed. I apologize for any wording that I have used that came from others but I may have forgotten the source.

Special thanks to:
My wife Donna, who gave faithful support, suggestions and prayers for the completion of this book.

I owe a debt of gratitude to our many friends and prayer groups for their prayers, counsel, support and encouragement.

The following people facilitated the publishing of this manuscript by organizing, outlining, critiquing, editing and formatting. Allow me to extend a very heartfelt "thank you" for the sacrifices made.

Linda Perry	David Herin
Wendy Beckett	Scott Keisler
Ron McDaniel	Rabbi Jeff Adler
Al Stevenson	Tom Davey
Debra Minotti	Zyrek Castelino
Stephen Briggs	Michael DeGrave
Gary Kah	

Preface

"Why another book on Israel?" you may ask. At the dawn of the information age, most Christians already seem laden with information overload and even prophetic burnout.

Well, this book focuses on an extremely important but neglected subject—a God-given burden of mine, conceived in my heart over the past several years. I trust it will be a wake-up call to the church that will stir, enlighten and challenge you to action and involvement. Paul, in Romans 11:17–21, warned the church in Rome not to be conceited and boastful over the natural branches (Israel) that were in part broken off:

> [17] And if some of the branches were broken off, and you, being a wild olive tree, were grafted in among them, and with them became a partaker of the root and fatness of the olive tree, [18] do not boast against the branches. But if you do boast, remember that you do not support the root, but the root supports you. [19] You will say then, "Branches were broken off that I might be grafted in." [20] Well said. Because of unbelief they were broken off, and you stand by faith. Do not be haughty, but fear. [21] For if God did not spare the natural branches, He may not spare you either.

Paul did not want the Church to be ignorant of the mystery of Israel. Yet by the third and fourth centuries, the dominant gentile church had disregarded all of Paul's warnings, rejecting the Jews as recipients of a future restoration God had promised. In so doing, the Church foolishly rejected her own Jewish roots, cutting itself out of the Jewish olive tree. The blessing ceased. The dark ages moved in and revelation lights faded out. Worse still, Replacement Theology[1] birthed virulent anti-Semitism[2] and the cross became a vicious sword.

Blood baths against the Jews throughout the Crusades[3], Inquisitions[4], Russian Pogroms[5] and the Holocaust[6] taint and mar Church history. At the hand of a 95% "Christian" nation, Nazi Germany slaughtered two-thirds of Europe's Jews. Nazis wore the Iron Cross[7] as a medal of valor, as though God Himself endorsed their savage genocidal program. Such atrocities committed under the sign of the cross, whether tacitly or overtly, created a barrier in the hearts and minds of the Jewish people. Tragically, this barrier against the church and Jesus Christ, the Jewish Messiah, is still present today.

Christianity began as a sect of Judaism with a Jewish Savior. How could such hatred have developed towards Israel? The cross, a symbol of God's love, literally became a sword, a symbol of hatred.

In solving a problem, understanding the problem is the first major step towards creating a genuine solution. In this book, I identify the following problems: wrong attitudes, actions, and Biblical blindness on the part of the church towards Israel. Having identified the true nature of the problem, I then offer clear-cut corrective action.

As you read this book, it may change your mind as preconceived ideas are dismantled and worldviews are changed. As you come to a compassionate awareness of the plight of the Jewish nation throughout history, I pray that incorrect and sinful attitudes will be adjusted.

The pages that follow present a challenging journey, but I hope that the journey will become a humbling experience that moves many to repentance. For too long we, as Christians, have been prideful, arrogant, conceited, and/or passive toward Israel and the Jewish people.

This message may hit a raw nerve. Comfort zones may be threatened. However, I am hopeful that many will make a decision to become involved and accountable.

My purpose in writing this study is not to teach a routine history lesson, nor do I intend to impose guilt upon anyone. My heart's desire is to impart a sense of awareness and responsibility to the reader.

[1] Replacement Theology—Another theological name is Supersessionism (There are variations of this theology)

- Israel (the Jewish people and the land) has been replaced by the Christian Church in the purposes of God, or, more precisely, the Church is the historic continuation of Israel to the exclusion of the Jewish people and their land.
- The Jewish people are now no longer a "chosen people." In fact, they are no different from any other group, such as the English, Spanish, or Africans.
- Apart from repentance, the new birth, and incorporation into the Church, the Jewish people have no future, no hope, and no calling in the plan of God. The same is true for every other nation and group.
- Since Pentecost of Acts 2, the term "Israel," as found in the Bible, now refers to the Church.
- The promises, covenants and blessings ascribed to Israel in the Bible have been taken away from the Jews and given to the Church, which has superseded them. However, the Jews are subject to the curses found in the Bible, as a result of their rejection of Christ.

[2] Anti-Semitism—hostility toward or discrimination against Jews as a religious, ethnic, or racial group.

[3] Crusades—any of the military expeditions undertaken by Christian powers in the 11th, 12th, and 13th centuries to win the Holy Land from the Muslims. Muslims and Jews were targets as they were both considered heretics and thereby imposters in the Holy Land.

[4] Inquisition—A Roman Catholic tribunal for discovery and punishment of heresy [of the Jews], which was marked by the severity of questioning and punishment and lack of rights afforded to the accused. While many people associate the Inquisition with Spain and Portugal, it was actually instituted by Pope Innocent III (1198–1216) in Rome.

[5] Pogroms—An organized, often officially encouraged massacre or persecution of a minority group, especially one conducted against Jews.

[6] Holocaust—The Holocaust was the systematic, bureaucratic, state-sponsored persecution and murder of approximately six million Jews by the Nazi regime and its collaborators. "Holocaust" is a word of Greek origin meaning "sacrifice by fire."

[7] Iron Cross—A military medal, the highest decoration for bravery awarded to the German armed forces in wartime. About 4.5 million were worn by the military. It was worn by all Nazis that carried out the Holocaust.

Introduction

Throughout history, there have been satanic attempts to exterminate the Jews by many peoples, nations, and religions. This important study will focus only on the hidden history of the Church's persecution of the Jewish people. *When the Cross Became a Sword* is but a brief overview and is not intended to be a comprehensive treatment. My aim is to paint a clear picture with "broad brush strokes."

I have included a bibliographical list of resources for those who wish to research and study the subject in more detail.

> . . .Write the vision and make it plain . . . that he
> may run who reads it. (Habakkuk 2:2)

This book covers the history of the Church from Rome to the Holocaust and beyond. The historic Church often embraced replacement theology—the belief that the original promises made by God to the children of Israel were nullified by Christ and that Israel is no longer God's chosen, covenant people. Thankfully, there has always been a small remnant who has loved and blessed the Jewish people, even when it was not popular to do so.

Yad Vashem, the Holocaust Memorial in Jerusalem, has a list of over 22,000 "Righteous Gentiles"[1] from 33 nations who helped Jews during the nightmare years of the Holocaust. Sadly however, Catholic and Protestant Christians constituted a small minority, compared to the millions of European Christians who were silent or even played a collaborative role with the Nazis.

We do not intend in this treatise to criticize or demean Church Fathers[2] and leaders of the past. Many, if not all, were leaders, theologians, and teachers of the Word of God. These were not evil men, and they most likely did not realize the consequences of their errors in interpreting Scripture, particularly with respect to God's irrevocable promises to the Jews and the future nation of Israel.

Please do not be offended by the historical facts presented here. These facts are intended to help us learn and move ahead so that we can avoid repeating similar mistakes in the future.

We desire to express love to the Jewish people, to call the Church to repentance for its anti-Semitic past and to help the Church understand God's eternal purposes for the Jewish people and the nation of Israel. Let us pray for revelation and a proper Scriptural understanding of the Church's relationship to Israel and the Jews.

In the words of scholar Edward Flannery:

> The vast majority of Christians, even well educated, are all but totally ignorant of what happened to Jews in history and of the involvement of the Church. . . . It is little exaggeration to state that those pages of history Jews have committed to memory are the very ones that have been torn from Christian (and secular) history books.

What a tragedy! We Christians are a people, redeemed by the Jewish Messiah and taught by Jewish prophets and the apostles. Our heritage is that of the Jewish people. We are grafted into Israel's olive tree (Romans 11:17). The Jewish Scriptures unite us. How could we be so uninformed regarding two thousand years of Jewish suffering? How could we have become such an instrument of destruction towards the Jewish people?

These "forgotten pages" of Church history, forgotten by our present generation and swept under the carpet cannot be ignored any longer simply because it is uncomfortable to deal with. I assure you that the Jewish people have not forgotten. Part of their God-given heritage is remembering their past.

Throughout the centuries, the Church openly taught that the Jews were the enemies of the cross. In the present generation, we ourselves have actively undermined the cross through Biblical ignorance. Sure we know about the Holocaust, but many of us are not aware that the anti-Semitic Church helped lay the foundation for the Nazis to build their doctrine. This is not an exaggeration.

Why and how could this happen? What went wrong? How could the historic "Church" get so far off course that she unmercifully slaughtered millions, for no other reason than being born a Jew?

We cannot correct the past wrongs but we certainly can do something about the present, and in so doing, we can help change the future and make restoration possible between the church, the Jews, and the nation of Israel.

---

[1] Righteous Gentiles—is the phrase used for those non-Jews who risked their lives to save Jews during the Holocaust.

[2] Church Fathers—any of about 70 theologians in the period from the 2nd to the 7th century whose writing established and confirmed official church doctrine.

From Error to Tragedy

To err is human but it can lead to dire consequences.

On September 1, 1983, a Korean airliner with 269 passengers departed from New York. After making a re-fueling stop in Anchorage, Alaska, the Boeing 747 took off for Seoul, South Korea. The pilot set the autopilot, targeting his flight pattern. However, minutes into the flight, the aircraft was diverging from its intended course. At first the error was negligible and not detected. As the plane veered off course, it entered Soviet airspace. By then it was too late to take corrective action. A Soviet MIG-23 fighter interceptor shot down flight 007 and all 269 passengers were lost. This tragedy began with a slight error, but the farther the plane went, the farther off course it became. Avoidable pilot error resulted in the needless loss of life.

Similarly, unbiblical error crept into the early Gentile Church, subtly at first. As the error matured, the Church veered more and more off course. By the time the error reached its logical conclusion, great, irreparable damage had already occurred. In the hidden pages of Church history, we discover a troubling and bloody legacy of hate that is still with us today. Modern day Jews still view the cross as a repugnant symbol of savagery, bigotry, and genocide.

Theological error known as "Replacement Theology"

Malcolm Hedding writes in his article, *Standing With Israel Today*:

> Replacement theology is nowhere to be found in the Bible. Those who hold to it do so merely based on a presupposition and nothing more. However, its destructive impact is all too clear.
>
> From a theological perspective, the Replacement doctrine can only exist if one can prove that the Abrahamic Covenant has been abolished.

Romans 9, 10, and 11

Art Katz said, "Untold numbers of ministers have gone their whole lifetime never having preached from these texts [Romans 9–11]. This is omitting the most critical, apostolic statement of the faith concerning God's purpose for both Israel and the Church."

Peter Tsukahira, in his book, *God's Tsunami*, writes about preachers of the Word who skip over Romans, Chapters 9, 10, and 11. He jokingly calls it "skipology." These three chapters are not parenthetical to what Paul had been teaching in Chapter 1–8 (as is often taught), nor are they merely something that Paul just "tacked on" to his teaching. They are the crux of the whole book of Romans! They reveal the "one new man," comprised of the Jewish believers (the cultivated olive tree) *and* Gentile believers (the wild olive branches grafted in). Krister Stendahl rightly points out that "Romans 9–11 is not an appendix to chapters 1–8, but the climax of the letter."

Paul wrote the book of Romans to the Church in Rome in about 54 A.D. The Roman Church was made up of primarily Gentile (non-Jewish) believers. By contrast, the Church birthed and headquartered in Jerusalem was primarily Jewish. Early

Jewish Christians gave their lives to bringing the gospel to the Gentiles—many became martyrs. By the early second century, for various reasons, the number of Jews in the young Church was decreasing while the number of Gentiles was greatly increasing. Gentiles were also assuming positions of leadership and influence within the Church.

Israel's Rejection—Not Total, Nor Final
Romans 11:

> ¹*I say then, has God cast away His people? Certainly not* . . .

> ¹¹*I say then, have they stumbled that they should fall? Certainly not!* But through their fall, to provoke them to jealousy, salvation has come to the Gentiles.

> ¹²Now if their fall is riches for the world, and their failure riches for the Gentiles, how much more their fullness!

> ¹⁵For if their being cast away is the reconciling of the world, what will their acceptance be but life from the dead?

> ¹⁶For if the first fruit is holy, the lump is also holy; and if the root is holy, so are the branches.

> ¹⁷And if some of the branches were broken off, *and you, being a wild olive tree, were grafted in among them and with them became a partaker of the root and fatness of the olive tree,*

Paul's Warning to the Gentiles Against Elitism and Exclusiveness

> ¹⁸*do not boast against the branches.* But if you do boast, remember that you do not support the root, but the root supports you.

> ¹⁹You will say then, "Branches were broken off that I might be grafted in."

²⁰Well said. Because of unbelief they were broken off, and you stand by faith. Do not be haughty, but fear.

²¹For if God did not spare the natural branches, He may not spare you either.

²²Therefore consider the goodness and severity of God: on those who fell, severity; but toward you, goodness, if you continue in His goodness. *Otherwise you also will be cut off.*

²³And they also, if they do not continue in unbelief, will be grafted in, for God is able to graft them in again.

²⁴For if *you were cut out of the olive tree which is wild by nature,* and were grafted contrary to nature into a cultivated olive tree, how much more will these, who are natural branches, be grafted into their own olive tree?

²⁵*For I do not desire, brethren, that you should be ignorant of this mystery, lest you should be wise in your own opinion . . .*

²⁶For the gifts and the calling of God are irrevocable. (Emphasis added)

As we will see, the Jewish Church was decreasing and the Church leadership fell into Gentile hands. Over the next few centuries, the Gentile Church violated every warning that Paul gave in Romans 11.

¹⁸*Do not boast* against the [natural] branches that were [in part] broken off . . .

²⁰. . . *Do not* be haughty but fear.

²⁵For I do not desire, brethren, that you should be *ignorant of this mystery [of Israel], lest you should be wise in your own opinion . . .* (Emphasis added)

We truly need to understand the "mystery of Israel"—past, present and future. However, we must not start in the middle of the Bible. We need to start at the beginning to avoid the error of "proof-texting."

The Apostle Paul taught that ignorance concerning God's plans and promises for Israel would lead the Gentiles to be wise in their own opinions. In other words, ignorance breeds pride and pride leads to hate. The fruits of ignorance are vanity, pride and arrogance.

Horace Mann said, "Ignorance breeds monsters to fill up the vacancies of the soul."

"For if *you were cut out of the olive tree which is wild by nature*, and were grafted contrary to nature into a cultivated olive tree, how much more will these, who are natural branches, be grafted into their own olive tree?" (Romans 11:24) (Emphasis added)

What is the major difference between the "wild olive branches" and the "natural branch-es?" The "wild olive branches" are the Gentile Christians from the New Testament era to the present time who were grafted into the olive tree. They did not have the same perspective as the Hebrew believers. Consequently, they could not fully appreciate or identify with the Jews and the Jewish Scriptures, written by the Jews, to the Jews in a Jewish culture. To truly understand the Old and New Testament scriptures, one needs to interpret the Scripture from a Hebraic perspective.

The "natural branches," or the Jewish people, understood Scripture from a Hebraic perspective. Their roots were ground-ed in the Jewish festivals, the Jewish community, and the com-ing Jewish Messiah who would fulfil all the Old Testament prophecies. The early New Testament Church was made up of Jewish people, with their roots still established in the fertile soil of first-century Judaism. The Jewish Apostles who penned the

New Testament were intimately familiar with Judaic customs and traditions.

We, as the Church, need to recapture the richness found in the roots of the Jewish olive tree. Our perspective needs to be that of the Hebrew people. This will enrich our view of Jesus and of the Scriptures. We need to view the prophecies concerning the return of the people of Israel to the land of their heritage from a Biblical perspective. This will resolve inaccurate theological views that come about when we interpret Scripture through the lens of Greek and gentile points of reference.

If you look at the real world of nature through a red lens, everything colored blue will look black. I liken this to interpreting Scripture through the distorting lens of false presuppositions. To say that God has rejected the Jewish people—that He has revoked His covenants and promises concerning their restoration to a prophetic role and destiny, transferring all these blessings to the Church—is to turn that which the Bible says is blue into something black.

The Western belief system is very different from the Eastern belief system. Western thought is not necessarily wrong, but when it comes to understanding Scripture, God has never endorsed uniting His ways with the ways of the world.

God chose Israel to be His people. Because of this, He also chose their culture, their concepts and their language to communicate His message. The Holy Spirit inspired the writing of the Scriptures. The message we have received derives (humanly speaking) from a Hebrew world of thought. As we interpret Scripture today, we must look at it with "Hebrew eyes" and with respect for the cultural context through which the revelation has been communicated.

The Hebrew mindset[1] is so foreign to us in the West that we find it difficult to comprehend. We quickly revert to our comfort zones in our study of the Scriptures. Consequently, we distort the intended Jewish viewpoint of the New Testament Scriptures. With an incomplete scriptural perspective, the Western mind (shaped by Greek philosophy) will naturally interpret the promised restoration of Israel in the last days through the false lens of allegory and spiritualization. The result is that the Church is viewed as the New Israel (Justin Martyr, 160 A.D.). Our prejudice distorts our perspective.

Robert Stearns says,

> . . . our faith is founded upon Judaism. The gospel is a Jewish message about a Jewish Messiah given to Jewish disciples within a Jewish context. The Bible tells us that salvation is "of the Jews" (John 4:22) and to them "pertain the adoption, the glory, the covenants . . ." (Romans 9:4). To not understand where they have come from is to not understand who we are or where we are going.

The Greek and the Hebrew mind both look at the same Scriptures and come to different conclusions. Both minds have a preconceived bias. The non-Jews of the Greco-Roman[2] world had an entirely different cultural legacy and perspective. They used different methods of interpretation with respect to the Jewish Scriptures.

Dr. David L. Cooper, Hebrew scholar, gave the golden rule of Biblical literal interpretation[3]:

> When the plain sense of Scripture makes common sense, seek no other sense; therefore, take every word at its primary, ordinary, usual literal meaning unless the facts of the immediate context, studied in the light of related passages and axiomatic and fundamental truths, indicate clearly otherwise.

When the Bible uses an allegory or figure of speech, it is usually obvious. But when an interpreter arbitrarily takes a passage that is obviously intended to be a literal statement of fact, and treats it as allegory, he is twisting the Word of God and knowingly perverting its meaning.

The Holy Spirit must be our guide

The Holy Spirit must be our guide as we study the Word of God. We must humble ourselves to the point of total dependence on Him and take Scripture at face value. To needlessly allegorize Scripture (a method introduced by Origen in the fourth century A.D.) is to begin the inevitable process of undermining the Scripture. We must not try to make Scripture fit neatly into our own presuppositions or doctrinal agendas. By allegory we can make it say whatever we want it to.

Ask yourself, what is your approach to Biblical thought? Are we to understand the Bible through the eyes of Hellenism[4] (Greek thought and culture) or through the eyes of Judaism (Hebrew thought and culture)?

As we will see, the historic Gentile Church, including the Church of Rome, answered this question incorrectly. This error took the Church, like the Korean airliner, tragically off course.

---

[1] Hebrew mindset—A worldview seeking to read and understand the Bible from the Hebrew setting, culture and traditions in which it was written.

[2] Greco-Roman—relating to both Greek and Roman thought.

[3] Literal Interpretation—Interpretation of scripture without allegorizing or spiritualizing, so that the sincere Bible student might resist conforming the Scriptures to any preconceived, theological conclusion; as well as ascertain what God Himself has desired to communicate to us in His written Word. An impossible goal apart from a consistent, literal interpretation of the Scriptures.

[4] Hellenism—Word used to express the assimilation, of Greek speech, manners, and culture, from the fourth century B.C. through the first centuries of the Common Era.

CHAPTER TWO

The Transition Era: From Jewish to Gentile

"If the church had paid attention to Paul's warnings in Romans 11, history would have been very different."

ANONYMOUS

In 70 A.D. Jerusalem was destroyed, including the Holy Temple, and the Jewish people were scattered to the four corners of the earth. During the dispersion, as the Jewish Christians (Messianic Believers) went into exile, their movement soon lost its Jewishness and evolved into a Gentile Christianity without Jewish roots.

A few decades later, the Bar Kochba Revolt against the Romans occurred (132 to 136 A.D.). By the end of the revolt, the Church had lost its Jewish leadership. A dramatic change took place and, in a short time Gentile leaders emerged.

In 135 A.D., Hadrian expelled all Jews from the city of Jerusalem, the Holy City was destroyed and decimated. Gentile cities like Alexandria, Rome, and Antioch soon became the centers of power and influence for the Christian faith. No longer was Jerusalem the headquarters of the Christian Church. The movement, once mostly Jewish, had now become mostly Gentile.

By the end of the second century, the shift was all but complete. The Church was reaching further into the Roman Empire and was progressively becoming a Greco-Roman institution. Greek and Roman influence crept into Biblical interpretation and a sweeping transformation was the outcome. As Replacement Theology emerged, heresies also arose. Sadly, these errors and the resulting heresies are still prevalent in Christian theology today.

As Greek philosophy infiltrated the Roman Church (for example the Platonism[1] and the neo-Platonsim[2] of Augustine, and later the Aristotelian ideas of Thomas Aquinas), it was becoming more Gentile-led and Gentile-bred. Non-Jewish Church Fathers were no longer feeding on the nourishing sap of the Jewish olive tree. Detachment set in and darkness soon followed. The glow of revelation burned out and the horrendous Dark Ages moved in.

Dr. Michael Brown, in his book, *Our Hands Are Stained With Blood*, states,

> The Dark Ages of the Church were the days of her greatest theological ignorance of Israel as well as the times of her most violent hostility toward the Jews.

---

[1] Platonism—A "school" of thought prominent in antiquity from the time of the founder Plato 428–348 B.C., up until at least the middle of the 6th century A.D. Platonism was unquestionably the dominant philosophical position in the ancient world over a period of more than 800 years.

[2] Neo-Platonism—a philosophical system originated in Alexandria in the 3rd century A.D., founded on Platonic doctrine.

CHAPTER THREE

Wrong Theology Leads to Anti-Jewish Bias

"Our bias distorts our perceptions that lead to error."

The allegorical[1] method of Bible interpretation soon became the recognized standard as the Church spread further into Gentile populations. This major shift led to serious inaccuracy in translating the Bible throughout the Church age. We need to restore the standard of literal Bible interpretation in our Churches and seminaries while we simultaneously emphasize the Hebraic context from which the Scriptures derive.

We must follow clear guidelines for interpreting Scripture today. The Hebrew context must always be the lens we use to study the Bible. Additionally, as a rule we must practice literal interpretation unless there is a compelling reason from the text itself not to do so. There are figurative statements in the Bible, of course, but even then the symbolism is often used to portray literal events.

Unfortunately, the early Church fathers did not always follow these rules. Rather than using a rule of literal interpretation, they often allegorized and spiritualized large amounts of text, with strange results. Furthermore, they failed to consult the historical and cultural Hebraic context of passages as they attempted to rightly divide the Word of Truth. Institutionalized anti-Semitism was the result.

An increasing anger toward the Jews developed in the writings of the Church fathers. When the allegorical method of interpretation is used, it denies the literal meaning of the text. Then you can make the text mean anything you want it to mean. This resulted in arriving at conclusions that grew from their own imaginations. This system produced the teaching that the Church is the "New Israel" of God. It replaced literal Israel in God's plan and purposes.

The Greek-inspired Church Fathers used the Scriptures to pronounce judgment and curses on Israel, yet applied the blessings spiritually to the Church. Hence, when the Church began to curse Israel, the Church opened itself up to curses, deception and blindness.

Hal Lindsey, in his book *The Road to Holocaust*, points out that the error was often unintended:

> The false form of the Church emerged through wrong theology initiated by men who were not evil. The early Church Fathers, like Origen and Augustine, had no idea of the far-reaching implications of their errors, especially in the area of prophecy.

As we will see, by the end of the third century, the image of the Jew was one of an unbeliever and a competitor. By the end of the fourth century, the Jew became the Christ killer, a satanic tool, cursed by God and discriminated against by the State. The very term "Jew" was an insult.

The following quotes are from Church Fathers of the second and third centuries who, with their presuppositions and the Greek philosophical approach to translation, took the Church off course. At first, the errors were gradual, but as time went on, the resulting consequences gained momentum. Eventually, destruction of millions of Jews resulted under the banner of the cross.

Justin Martyr (100–165 A.D.) was the earliest apologetic writer of the Church who wrote in the mid-first century his Dialogue with Trypho the Jew, ". . . the Jews have forfeited the Scriptures, and the prophets are now the property of the Church. . . ." This is believed to be the first written example of Replacement Theology.

Ignatius of Antioch (martyred 117 A.D.) contended that the Jews were in league with the devil and warned his readers to be on their guard against their evil practices.

The Gospel of Barnabas (130 A.D.) warns its audience against the Jews and states that the Jews have "lost" the covenants.

An early accusation of deicide[2] (Christ killers) was put forward by Melito of Sardis (d. 190 A.D.), who accused the Jews of sending Jesus to the cross, and therefore of being directly responsible for the death of God.

Clement of Alexandria (150–215 A.D.) emphasized Greek philosophy rather than the Tanakh as the primary means God gave the Gentiles to lead them to Jesus as the ultimate "Word of God." He blended Greek philosophy with Christianity to make Christianity acceptable to the Gentiles. It is said that Clement was more comfortable with Plato than he was with Moses. This resulted in his students looking more to Athens than to Jerusalem.

Hippolytus (160–236 A.D.), in his *Expository Treatise Against the Jews* also placed the charge of deicide on the Jews.

He proclaimed that the Jewish people were a perverse race, as could be seen in the way they glorified in the sufferings of the death of Jesus.

Tertullian (160–220 A.D.), as a prolific writer, joined his voice with others, in his *Answer to the Jews*—he presented the Jews as idolaters.

Origen (185–253 A.D.) is credited with being the father of the allegorical method of interpretation. The reason is that Origen, in a comprehensive system, made allegory the only way to truly understand the Scriptures. His knowledge of philosophy and theology brought him fame and influence throughout the Roman world, even by the Emperor. Origen's students became leading theologians using his allegorical method of interpretation of the Scriptures. This helped to establish it as official Church teaching, also laying the foundations for anti-Semitism in the Church, which only gained momentum in successive generations.

Eusebius (263–339 A.D.) was considered a "Father of Church History." He played a leading role of influence along with Emperor Constantine, at the Council of Nicea (325 A.D.), which was attended by 318 bishops, none of whom were Jewish believers. They decided to separate Easter from Passover. Constantine considered it unbecoming beyond measure that Christians were following the practices of this "most odious" people and were unable to celebrate their festival(s) without the aid of their rules.

Eusebius wrote that the promises of the Hebrew Scriptures were for Christians and not the Jews, and the curses were for the Jews. He argued that the Church was the continuation of the Old Testament and thus superseded Judaism. The young Church declared itself to be the true Israel, or "Israel according to the Spirit"—heir to the divine promises. They found it essential to discredit the "Israel according to the flesh" to prove that God had cast away His people and transferred His love to the Christians.

Eusebius may be credited with the notion that the heroes of the Old Testament were not Jews but, in fact, proto-Christians. It is interesting that the false prophet Mohammed picked up this idea when he claimed that the Patriarchs were not Jewish but were "hanif"[3] or proto-Moslems.

Replacement Theology originated when Greek interpretation suppressed the Hebrew mindset of the Scriptures. The Gentile Church then became the dominant influence. This was the basis for the foundation of anti-Semitism, which exists to this day, even within some churches. The New Testament states that the Gentile believers were grafted in and became the sons of Abraham and spiritual Israel. However, we should not presume that the God-given covenants of the Jewish nation now belong to the Church and that the Church has replaced physical Israel. This wrong theology eventually steered the Church off course from the Apostles' original instructions found in New Testament scripture.

Ephraem Syrus (306–373 A.D.) used language that became common usage when referring to the Jews. He described the Jewish people as harlots and prostitutes, concluding, "Israel is wanton between the legs."

Athanasius of Alexandria (296–373 A.D.) was a fourth-century leader and formulator of creeds, considered that the Roman Empire should take up the "Sword of Judgment" against the Jews.

Gregory of Nissa (d. 394 A.D.) described the Jews as murderers, rebels, and detesters of all that was good. He proclaimed that the Jews were companions of the devil and were a Sanhedrin of demons.

John Chrysostom, much admired Bishop of Constantinople (345–405 A.D.), was, and still is, considered one of the greatest orators of all time. In a well-known series of eight popular sermons entitled *Against the Jews*, he wrote scathing denunciations of the Jews and their synagogues. He called their synagogues brothels, a criminal's hangout, a resort of demons, a citadel of the devil, the ruin of souls, and a pit of destruction. He described the Jews as no better than goats or hogs. At the end of the series, he encouraged his listeners to make an active response against the enemies of Christ. He contended, "God has always hated the Jews [and] it is incumbent upon all Christians to hate the Jews." His sermons were put in written form and were widely circulated. His verbal attacks were the most vicious of the early Church Fathers. His sermons fanned the flames of anti-Semitism that became the official teaching and practice of the Church.

In the fifth century, the Roman State Church viewed the Jews as second-class citizens who were forever marked and branded as outcasts from the normal order of society. This anti-Semitic attitude of the powerful Roman State/Church laid the foundation for the future of the Jews, as they would experience unbelievable suffering and persecution for the next 1500 years.

As Christianity spread, more and more countries came under the influence of the Roman Church, spreading the anti-Jewish attitudes and policies that came out of the Roman world.

To the list is added:

Ambrose of Milan (339–397 A.D.), who viewed the Jews as the enemies of Christ and instigated riots and acts of destruction against Jewish communities.

Cyril of Alexandria (376–444 A.D.) was the pope of Alexandria for many years. He was not opposed to acts of extreme violence against perceived enemies; among them the Jews were significant. He considered the Jews to be on the same level as pagans and had them expelled from the city.

Jerome (360–420 A.D.), considered a Saint, wrote comments in his Tractate against the Jews. It was understood by some to have been grounds for forced conversions. This set a pattern for the next thousand years of attempts of forced conversion campaigns.

Augustine of Hippo (354–430 A.D.) considered the true image of the Jew was Judas Iscariot. He believed the Jews were incapable of understanding the Scriptures and would therefore eternally bear the responsibility for the death of Jesus. He believed that the Jews were completely evil and drew conclusions that the Jews are dirt under Gentile feet. Augustine's writings became the theological textbook for the Church and his views are still being taught today.

Avitus, Bishop of Clermont (470–485 A.D.), took a reactive role against the Jews in his area in 576 A.D. by setting the synagogue on fire and offering the Jews a choice between baptism and exile. "Ferréol ordered the Jews of his diocese to meet in the Church of St. Theodoric, and preached to them a baptismal sermon. Some Jews abjured [denied] their faith; he forbade the others to remain in the city, and expelled them from his diocese" in 558 A.D. (Jewish Encyclopaedia).

---

[1] Allegorical Interpretation—places on biblical literature a meaning that, with rare exceptions, it was never intended to convey.

[2] Deicide—the killing of God or a god.

[3] Hanif—A pre-Islamic (Arabian) monotheist whose beliefs are thought to have descended from the time of the *hanif* Abraham, independently of Judaism.

CHAPTER FOUR

The Middle Ages: The Cross Became a Sword

The time of Constantine in the fourth century A.D. to the First Crusade in 1096 A.D. is known as the Middle Ages or the Dark Ages. When the predominately Gentile Church, gaining in power and influence, began to reject its Jewish roots, the "lights" went out. They were cutting themselves off from the Jewish olive tree, as illustrated in the figure below.

The Dark Ages set in, a dark era indeed for Jews in the "Christian" Roman Empire. It was during this time that the cross became a sword!

At the beginning of the fourth century, after a period of persecution involving key Church leaders, the Roman Emperor Constantine became the first Christian Roman Emperor in 306 A.D. In 313 A.D. the Edict of Milan legalized Christianity, returned property to many churches, even offering the churches the protection of the State. Though scholars debate the authenticity of Constantine's conversion, the net effect was that Christianity became the official religion of the Roman Empire. But the new state religion endorsed Replacement Theology. This meant the end of formal persecution of Christians, but it also meant the beginning of persecution of the Jewish people in the name of the Church!

Constantine's reformation in the image of the Greek mindset officially laid the groundwork for the age of Neo-Platonism. Constantine was unquestionably the political impetus behind sweeping ecclesiastical transformation, but it was Augustine of Hippo (354–430 A.D.) who laid the theological and philosophical groundwork for a new era in Christendom. Although it is admittedly an oversimplification, it can be said that Augustine injected Plato into Christian theology, and Thomas Aquinas injected Aristotle at the dawn of the new millennium.

A "Christianized" form of Plato's philosophy ultimately completely displaced a Hebrew-centered understanding of the Scriptures. At this point, Plato's abjectly pagan philosophy became the grid for all interpretation of the Bible. The Jewishness of sacred Scripture was lost.

That is not to say that there were no bright spots. Many Latin-speaking Christians in the Western Roman Empire strongly resisted the insertion of Greek philosophy into theology. Tertullian, for example, famously posed this question:

"What hath Athens to do with Jerusalem, or the academy with the Church?" Unfortunately, Christians like Tertullian who opposed such changes were often subject to exile or death.

Constantine was severely anti-Jewish before he confessed he was a Christian. His anti-Semitism did not disappear the moment of his conversion. In fact, Constantine pressed the scholars and leaders of his era to purge the Church of all remaining vestiges of Jewish concepts and practices.

Paganism Pollutes Christianity

During the first two centuries after Christ, persecution of the Christians in Rome had been severe. Many of the Gentile believers and most of the Jewish Christians suffered martyrdom for their faith. Fortunately—for the Christians anyway—this changed early in the fourth century, during the era of Constantine.

When Constantine converted to Christianity, a major turning point occurred in the history of the Church. Historians can only speculate as a motive of his conversion, whether sincere or political. But either way, the result was the same. The rise of a Christian Emperor halted the persecution of Christians and initiated Christendom into the Roman Empire.

However, Constantine's burgeoning Church State, with Augustine providing the intellectual support, completely severed the Church from its Jewish roots. Christian Rome ended the usage of the Jewish calendar, including Jewish Sabbaths and festivals. The Roman calendar we still use today was the result. Scripture was filtered almost exclusively through a Greco-Roman paradigm. Church government, architecture, scriptural date keeping, doctrines and Church life changed radically.

The sword of the state enforced the new laws in Constantine's edict. These horrific laws, requiring separation from the Jews and compelling the Christians to hate them, established official state-sponsored anti-Semitic policies. This was the only attitude to be accepted by the Christians toward the Jewish people. If any Jews converted to Christianity, they had to renounce their Jewish customs and conform to the Gentile pattern of Christianity.

David Stern, in his book *Restoring the Jewishness of the Gospel*, gives the following profession from the Church of Constantinople—required of all Jews who accepting Jesus as their Messiah and wishing to join the Church:

> I renounce all customs, rites, legalisms, unleavened breads and sacrifice of lambs of the Hebrews, and all the other feasts of the Hebrews, sacrifices, prayers, aspersions, purifications, sanctifications and propitiations, and fasts, and new moons, and Sabbaths, and superstitions, and hymns and chants and observances and synagogues, and the food and drink of the Hebrews.
>
> In one word, I renounce absolutely everything Jewish, every law, rite and custom—and if afterwards I shall wish to deny and return to Jewish superstition, or shall be found feasting with Jews, or secretly conversing and condemning the Christian religion instead of openly confuting them and condemning their vain faith, then let the trembling of Cain and the leprosy of Gehazi cleave to me, as well as the legal punishments to which I acknowledge myself liable. And may I be anathema in the world to come, and may my soul be set down with Satan and the devils.

Under Constantine, the institutional Church merged with the State. The Roman Empire became Christian Rome. Within the century Augustine provided intellectual support in favor of the Church-State model while injecting Platonism and Neo-Platonism into Christian Theology. Furthermore, the wildly influential Augustine was not averse to Origen's allegorical methods of Scriptural interpretation.

The Roman State Church considered itself the Kingdom of God on earth, and it had the political and military might of the Roman Empire backing it up. Sadly, the emerging medieval Church bore little resemblance to the early first-century Church. It is not too much to say that the early apostles would not have recognized the Church in her new form.

Throughout history, the union of Church and state has led to corruption and death. It was never God's plan for this age.

CHAPTER FIVE

The Medieval Period to the Crusades

The medieval Crusades were holy wars. Initially, only expeditions sanctioned by the Pope to the Holy Land (Israel and Jerusalem) were considered "official" crusades. The pope's armies fought against groups viewed as enemies of Christendom. There were unofficial Crusades as well.

The Crusades, called in the name of Christ, remain one of the darkest stains in the history of the Church. Pope Urban II initiated the Crusades on November 27, 1095. The purpose was to recover the Holy land from the Moslems and stop the spread of Islam. These "Christian" Crusades took place during the eleventh, twelfth, and thirteenth centuries. There were a total of seven, or possibly eight (depending upon whom you ask). According to their "replacement theology," the Holy Land and Jerusalem, its capital, belonged to the Church. Moslems and Jews were considered heretics usurping Christian land.

Yet the Lord refers to Jerusalem and that area as "His" land. Joel 3:2 is just one reference. And the Lord gives the land to whom He pleases. In the irrevocable Abrahamic covenant (Genesis 12, 15, 17), God gave the land of Israel to the Jewish people forever.

> To all the land which you see, to you will I give it, and to your descendants forever (Genesis 13:15).

Many of the Crusaders were sincere, but misguided Christians. The Crusades were viewed as an opportunity to kill heretics and plunder them in the name of God—having their sins forgiven by the Pope in the process.

In the First Crusade (1096–99 A.D.), deicide (Jews as the Christ killers) was widely accepted as just cause for the extermination of the Jews, wherever they were. The Crusaders not only hated the Moslems, but they hated the Jews. The First Crusade destroyed European Jewish communities along the Rhine and Danube Rivers with ferocity.

Before departing on the Crusade, Godfrey de Bouillon, the first Crusader King, proclaimed he would avenge the blood of Christ on Israel and leave no member of the Jewish race alive.

The Crusaders murdered the Jews wherever they could be found, destroying the long-established Jewish communities of Speyer, Mainz and Worms. They savagely killed thousands of Jews, all done under the banner of the cross and in the name of Christ.

The Jews have not forgotten these atrocities committed by so-called Christians. Perhaps the worst act of infamy took place in Jerusalem on July 15, 1099 A.D., where Jews were hoarded together like cattle and locked in a synagogue. With the doors and windows barred, Jews inside were exterminated alive by fire. Horrifically, the Crusaders—crosses on their shields and breastplates—enjoyed the spectacle, singing "Christ, We Adore Thee" as they watched.

Jews Blamed for the Plague of the Black Death

Approximately 25 million died during the Black Death plague between 1347–1350 A.D. — up to half of Europe's population. Medieval Europe was replete with Biblical illiteracy, spiritual ignorance, and superstition. The caricature of the Jew as an agent of the devil was all too easily accepted by religious Europeans. As the Black Death raged on out of control, the masses blamed Jews for poisoning the wells. As a result, Jews were executed *en masse*.

The Beginning of Jewish Ghettos[1]

In 1222 A.D., in a move to prevent defilement of churches by the presence of Jews, the Provincial Synod of Canterbury made a ruling that forbade Jewish people from entering Christian places of worship.

Vincent Ferrer (1350–1419 A.D.), a Dominican friar and preacher, practiced forced-conversion of the Jews. Along with a band of 300 followers, he would enter a town during a time of Jewish worship, burst into a synagogue, and demand the Jews accept conversion. Ferrer, in fact, was the leading influence behind the Edict of Castile (January 14, 1412), which contained 24 articles against the Jews and established the creation of ghettos in all Spanish towns.

Pope Paul IV (1476–1559 A.D.) issued an edict directing the establishment of ghettos throughout Catholic Europe. Paul's successor, Pius V (1504–1572 A.D.), took the measures one step further, expelling Jews from three Papal States.

The Beginning of Distinctive Markings on Clothing

The Fourth Lateran Council (1215 A.D.) was responsible for the Distinctive Clothing Order. Wearing distinct badges on their outer garments, representing the areas where they lived, Jews were humiliated and identified as a danger to society. This of course, was a forerunner to the "yellow star of David" that Nazi Germany required the Jews to wear in the twentieth century. Sadly we must confess that the Church was responsible for setting this precedent.

---

[1] Ghetto—a quarter of a city in which Jews were formerly required to live.

CHAPTER SIX

The Spanish Inquisition

The Spanish Inquisition, the most deadly inquisition in history, began on November 1, 1478 A.D. and lasted until 1492. There are no accurate records of how many Jews were executed at the hands of the Spanish Inquisition, but many scholars and experts believe several thousand Jews were killed.

The Inquisition forced Jews to be baptized and convert to Roman Catholicism. Refusal meant the loss of property, exile, or even death. If a Jew accepted baptism, they had to renounce their Jewishness. If a Jew refused baptism, his property was confiscated and sold to the highest bidder. If the Jew was lucky enough not to be executed, he was forced into exile.

There were many converts *(Conversos)*, who upon threat of death, recanted their Jewishness and accepted Catholic baptism. Many Jews converted to Christianity to avoid persecution but continued to practice their religion secretly. As result, they were referred to as *Marranos*, a derogatory Spanish word meaning "pig."

According to the chronicler Andreas Bernfeldez, in the seven years between 1481 and 1488 the Inquisition found many of the Conversos guilty of practicing Judaism. They burned 700 at the stake, while 5,000 recanted their "backsliding." A steady stream of Spanish Jews was brought before the Inquisitors for committing the crime of people celebrating Jewish festivals, owning Hebrew Scriptures, and circumcising children.

Bernard Gui wrote a manual for carrying out the Inquisition. This manual provided a long list of hints on how to spot a Jew or a backsliding convert. The manual also included methods of extracting confessions from the suspects under interrogation, including:

- The needle

- The whip, (Flagellation): Whipping was a common practice in medieval times.

- The flame, torture by fire, was probably the most painful and excruciating form of torture.

- The garrotte in which a tightened iron collar is used to strangle or break the neck of a condemned person.

- The rack was one of the most well-known forms of medieval torture. This pain inducing mechanism worked by having the victim lie on a horizontal rack with his hands and ankles tied to rollers on opposite ends. The Inquisitors would perform the interrogation while turning the rollers, stretching the body of the suspect and causing colossal pain. They would stretch the body out until the joints were actually yanked from their sockets, with the ultimate intent of killing the victim either through shock or injuries.

Peter de Rosa, author of "Vicars of Christ: The Dark Side of the Papacy," wrote:

Of eighty popes in a line from the thirteenth century on, not one of them disapproved of the theology and apparatus of Inquisition. On the contrary, one after another added his own cruel touches to the workings of this deadly machine.

Seal for the Tribunal of the Holy Office
of the Inquisitor in Spain.
Notice the cross and the sword.

CHAPTER SEVEN

Anti-Semitism: Examples from Russian History

Russian Tsars, like Ivan IV (the Terrible), focused their attention on Jews, whom they considered the enemies of Christ. When Ivan's army occupied the Polish city of Polotzk in 1563, it had a large and prosperous Jewish community. The Orthodox Church ordered all local Jews to convert to the Orthodox faith. Those who resisted suffered the consequences: they were drowned in the Dvina River or burned at the stake.

From 1791 until 1915, the majority of Jews living in Eastern Europe were confined by the Czars of Russia to an area known as the "Pale of Settlement"[1] (meaning "borders of settlement"). The Pale was first created by Catherine the Great in 1791 to remove Jews from Russia entirely, unless they converted to Russian Orthodoxy, the state religion. The Jews of Russia were specifically expelled from Moscow and St. Petersburg and forced into the Pale. The Pale consisted of 25 provinces that included Ukraine, Lithuania, Belorussia, Crimea and part of Poland. The concentration of Jews in the

Pale made them easy targets for pogroms and anti-Jewish riots by the masses.

The Russian Orthodox Church played a major part in the persecution of the Jews. In fact, it added to the pogroms and encouraged the attacks. Konstantin Pobedonostev, the head of the governing body of this "Church" summed up their position in the May Laws (May 1882). He expressed hope that "one-third of Jews will convert, one-third will die and one-third will flee the country."

The Jews of Tsarist Russia were the victims of three large-scale waves of pogroms, each of which surpassed the preceding in scope and savagery. These pogroms consisted of targeted and repeated anti-Semitic rioting and violent mob attacks. These occurred between the years 1881 and 1884, 1903 and 1906, and then after the Russian Revolution, pogroms occurred from 1917 to 1921.

The pogroms between 1903–1906 left an estimated 2,000 Jews dead, with many more wounded. These deaths occurred as the Jews took to arms to defend their families and property from the attackers. The 1905 pogrom of Jews in Odessa was the most serious pogrom of the period, with reports of up to 2,500 Jews killed.

---

[1] Pale of Settlement—Throughout Russia's history, the czars refused all Jews entry into Russia. The First Partition of Poland, in 1772, brought hundreds of thousands of Jews into Russian territory. Russia's rulers decided to restrict Jews to certain geographical areas, thereby creating the Pale of Settlement. The original Pale, established in 1791, included modern Poland, Ukraine, Lithuania and Belarus. Within the Pale itself, Jews were denied higher education and land ownership. The setting for the movie, *Fiddler on the Roof*, took place in Ukraine during the Pale, possibly in the late 1800's and early 1900's.

CHAPTER EIGHT

Protestant Reformation:
Emerging From the Dark Ages

"How odd of God to choose the Jew!
But not as odd as those who choose the Jewish God, and hate the Jew!"
OGDEN NASH

The Renaissance and the Reformation brought no relief to the anti-Semitism within Christendom. Erasmus of Rotterdam (1466–1536 A.D.), in a letter to the Inquisitor of Cologne, wrote, "If it is Christian to hate Jews, here we are all Christians in profusion."

Anti-Semitism still permeated the theology of the reformers and affected their attitude toward the Jews. (Their attitudes were not much different from previous theology.)

The Protestant Reformation, led by Europeans like Martin Luther, renewed some of the cardinal teachings of the ancient Church and was a breath of fresh air to the Church. Luther did many great things, such as translating the Greek New Testament to German, the language of the common people. He also wrote some of the great hymns of the Church. The reformers read the Bible in a literal sense in many areas of theology and doctrine, but they continued to espouse Replacement Theology when it came to the relationship of the Church to the Jewish people and covenant Israel. (They also tended to allegorize prophetic Scriptures concerning end-time events.)

It is tragic that the anti-Jewish attitudes of his time continued to influence the great reformer Martin Luther. Early in his ministry, Luther wrote a very sympathetic tract acknowledging the shameful way the Church had treated the Jews. He urged kind and sympathetic treatment toward them. However, in his latter days, when the Jews did not embrace his new gospel message, he wrote another tract called *Concerning the Jews and Their Lies*. That tract was scathing, to say the least. In it he stated:

> . . . their synagogues should be set on fire . . . this should be done for the honor of God . . . their homes should be destroyed . . . they should be deprived of their prayer books . . . their Talmud teaches idolatry, lies, cursing and blasphemy . . . their rabbis must be forbidden under the threat of death to teach anyone . . . passports and traveling privileges should be absolutely forbidden to Jews . . . let us drive them out of our country for all time.

The Encyclopedia Judaica rightly comments about Luther's tract:

> Short of the Auschwitz oven and extermination, the whole Nazi Holocaust is pre-outlined here.

As a child, Adolph Hitler attended a Catholic school. The anti-Semitic concepts of the early Church fathers, including Martin Luther, fueled the flame of an intense hatred within him. In justifying his deplorable deeds of genocide, Hitler quoted Martin Luther to justify "The Final Solution[1] to the Jewish Problem."

Germany gave Hitler its highest award for bravery—the Iron Cross. The Catholic Church never excommunicated Hitler for what he did to the Jews.

Iron Cross—A military medal, the highest decoration for bravery awarded to the German armed forces in wartime.
About 4.5 million were worn by the military.
It was worn by all Nazis that carried out the Holocaust.

---

[1] Final Solution—"The Final Solution of the Jewish Question" also known as The Holocaust. An euphemistic name for both Nazi Germany's plan to completely annihilate all European Jews and their attempt to do so between 1941 and 1945.

CHAPTER NINE

The Holocaust: Hitler's "Final Solution"

"Nazi anti-Judaism was the work of godless, Anti-Christian criminals. But it would not have been possible without the almost two thousand years' pre-history of 'Christian' anti-Judaism."

HANS KUNG

Christians all over the world know about the Holocaust, but many are not aware of how deeply anti-Semitism exists in the Church. The Church laid the groundwork upon which the Nazis founded their doctrine.

Anti-Semitism did not just come into being spontaneously in 1933. The Nazi system did not materialize from a vacuum; it was the climax of pagan philosophy and church doctrine dating back to third century A.D. and earlier. Raul Hilberg in his book, The Destruction of the European Jews, states:

> Since the fourth century after Christ, there have been three anti-Jewish policies: conversion, expulsion and annihilation.

The missionaries of Christianity have said in effect: YOU HAVE NO RIGHT TO LIVE AMONG US AS JEWS.

The secular rulers who followed have proclaimed, YOU HAVE NO RIGHT TO LIVE AMONG US.

The German Nazis have at last decreed: YOU HAVE NO RIGHT TO LIVE.

This progressive hatred brought in its wake a slow and steady growth of anti-Jewish actions and anti-Jewish rational. We see then that the German Nazis did not discard the past in pursuit of a noble new idea; they built upon the foundation of an old idea deeply embedded in European culture. Fueled by the convenient and sympathetic philosophies of Hegel, Marx, Nietzsche, and social Darwinism, the Third Reich was able to justify the final solution, taking the anti-Semitic theology of Christian Europe to its logical conclusion.

One could argue that Adolf Hitler applied and exploited the historical hatred of Jews demonstrated time and time again by the European Church. Could it be that this is how he was able to write in *Mein Kampf*?

> "Hence today I believe that I am acting in accordance with the Almighty Creator: by defending myself against the Jew, I am fighting for the work of the Lord." (Adolf Hitler, *Mein Kampf*, translated by Ralph Manheim) (Boston: Houghton Mifflin Co. 1971, page 65).

From a pamphlet, *Glimpses of a People, Events, Life and Faith from the Church Across the Ages*, Issue #207, published by the Christian History Institute, we find these statistics:

- 95 per cent of Hitler's Germans declared themselves officially as Christian (Catholic or Protestant).

- During the first years of Hitler's rule, 95–98 per cent of this same population supported Nazi policies through regular referendum.

- In spite of his reservations, the Pope gave formal support to Hitler's government in 1933 by signing an agreement that promised Rome's support to Hitler so long as Hitler defended the Church.

- Hitler enjoyed widespread support from the Protestant churches. Eighty-five per cent of Protestant pastors took the oath of personal loyalty to Adolf Hitler (some under duress, but most willingly).

- As soon as Hitler took office in 1933, he began rounding up the Jews and thrusting them into concentration camps. These concentration camps became "death camps" by 1939. As Hitler broadened his reign throughout Europe, he herded the Jewish people like livestock by the trainload, transporting them from their homes to death camps.

- Hitler's plan was to eradicate the Jews totally from the face of the earth. Furthermore, he rationalized his plan by quoting Martin Luther. Hitler called this plan "The Final Solution to the Jewish Problem." History calls Hitler's "solution" the Holocaust.

Thankfully, there has always been a small remnant that has loved and blessed the Jewish people, even when it was neither popular nor safe to do so. The Holocaust Memorial in Jerusalem, Yad Vashem — one of the most popular tourist attractions in all of Israel — has a list of over 22,000 "Righteous Gentiles" from 33 nations who came to the aid of Jews during the nightmarish years of the Holocaust. These non-Jewish individuals risked life, liberty, and treasure in order to save the Jewish people.

Similarly, hundreds of pastors in Germany during the Third Reich refused to take the oath of loyalty to Hitler. It is estimated that 800 pastors were arrested and imprisoned for not accepting the Nazification of their churches.

Dietrich Bonheoffer in particular was one of the few church leaders who stood in courageous opposition to the Fuehrer and his xenophobic policies. In taking a stand, Bonheoffer laid down his life in martyrdom. Bonheoffer's prophetic words serve as an important reminder to the Body of Christ:

> "Silence in the face of evil is itself evil: God will not hold us guiltless. Not to speak is to speak. Not to act is to act."

The Hiding Place, the autobiography of Corrie ten Boom, relates why her family became rescuers of Jews in Holland and why they were willing to risk their lives. Corrie emphasizes in the book that the Old Testament was deeply cherished in her home growing up, adding that her family always felt a profound sense of religious kinship with the Jews. Corrie's father, Casper, often repeated his belief that the Jews were God's chosen people and "the apple of God's eye."

Corrie, in the shadow of World War II and anticipating the need to help Jews, prayed the following prayer:

> "Lord Jesus, I offer myself for Your people, in any way, any place and any time."

History records that the family perished, save only Corrie, who was unintentionally released due to a clerical error. She spent the last few years of her life telling the world about her family's love for the Jews.

During WWII, Polish Catholic Irena Sendler (1910-2008), using nursing credentials, received permission to work in the Warsaw Ghetto. Sendler smuggled more than 2,500 Jewish children out of Warsaw in various ways. Hiding the children in a Burlap sack in the back of her truck, she snuck the frightened children past the Nazis with a trained dog that would bark on command in order to cover up the sound of crying. She then provided those children with false identity documents and housing outside the Ghetto, thereby saving them from almost certain death at the hands of the Nazis. In 1943 Sendler was arrested by the Gestapo, severely tortured, and sentenced to death—only a bribe from an underground organization later saved her life. In her final years a child Sendler rescued from the Nazis cared for Sendler in a reciprocal act of mercy. In 2008, Sendler died in Warsaw at age 98.

Sadly however, these Catholic and Protestant Christians constituted a tiny minority, compared to the millions of European Christians who were either silent or played a collaborative role with the Nazis during the Holocaust years.

CHAPTER TEN

Twenty-First-Century Church

"The Jews are a nervous people.
Nineteen centuries of Christian love have taken a toll."
BENJAMIN DISRAELI

The Greco-Roman philosophy still lingers in some believers to-day—a hangover from the Dark Ages. We see it in our Church doctrine, practices, architecture, the arts and in our worldview. The effects of the Dark Ages have endured into the twenty-first century and will not go away until we do something about it. We must eradicate pagan philosophy from the grid through which we interpret Scripture. This in turn will affect our preaching, teaching, and our everyday walk with the Lord.

Replacement Theology has produced in the Church a blood-stained history. A dark cloud lingers over believers to this day. We, as Christians, must repent of this legacy of hate from our own past. I am not talking about a self-loathing guilt trip, but we need to hold ourselves accountable for the Church's mistakes—past and present.

Without a doubt, hatred of the Jews is on the rise again in this world. We must also be attentive to current events if we are to avoid repeating the sinful actions of the past.

Today the Jews are being re-gathered to their ancient home-land, Israel. Anti-Semitism in the Church is presently disguis-ing itself as anti-Zionism[1], which prevails not only among Arab Muslims, but also from "Christian" institutions—in-cluding mainline Protestant denominations, Roman Catholics, Orthodox, and pro-U.N. Liberal church and para-church or-ganizations like the World Council of Churches. Even some Reformed circles are vehemently anti-Israel.

At the same time, there is a growing number of Christians that believe in Zionism. Biblical Zionism is the firm belief that God chose the Jewish people and bequeathed to them as an everlasting possession the Land of Canaan. Zionism holds that the modern restoration of Israel is not a political anomaly, but evidence of God's ongoing faithfulness to His people with re-spect to His covenant made with the Patriarch Abraham.

> "And I will establish My covenant between Me and you and your descendants after you in their generations, for an everlasting covenant, to be God to you and your descendants after you. Also I give to you and your descendants after you the land in which you are a stranger, all the land of Canaan, as an everlasting possession; and I will be their God." (Genesis 17:7-8)

---

[1]Anti-Zionism—hostility toward or discrimination against Jews as a nation, religious, ethnic, or racial group.

CHAPTER ELEVEN

Recovering Our Jewish Roots

"Change takes but an instant,
resistance to change can last a lifetime."
JEWISH PROVERB

A deep-seated appreciation of our Jewish roots is necessary to give us a scriptural basis for what we believe in and abide by. We need to examine the Scriptures and try to comprehend in what manner the Jews have understood them throughout history, but especially in Biblical times. It will not be easy for us to achieve this standard of interpretation because in so many ways Greco-Roman paradigms are interwoven into the very fabric of our culture. For example, many of the philosophical and intellectual assumptions of Western culture are inherently Greek. Our legal structure is inherently Roman. What's more, as the United States and the Western world has drifted into a post-Christian society, on the heels of modernism and now post-modernism, in our morals and ethics, we have forgotten Jerusalem. Difficult as it may be, we must tirelessly endeavor—with the constant aid and tutelage of the Holy Spirit—recapture the inherent

Jewishness of the Scriptures and the richness of the Hebrew cultural context from which the Bible derives. As we begin to do this we will discover hidden treasures in the Scriptures and we will glimpse the fullness of Biblical truth God intended for His people.

Dr. John D. Garr, in his book, *Restoring Our Lost Legacy*, says,

> For the past nineteen centuries, millions of believers have been denied their biblical legacy, the riches of the Hebrew foundations of their faith. Christian Judaeophobia, anti-Judaism, and anti-Semitism have conspired to rob them of the treasures of their inheritance.

Mark Kinzer phrases it so well,

> Israel's covenant endures, the Church draws nourishment from its Jewish root, yet Yeshua [Jesus] remains the Messiah and Lord for both Jews and Gentiles. The Christian church can now affirm its own identity as an extension of Israel in a non-supersessionist manner. . . . The church must reckon with the subtle ways it has lost touch with its own identity as a Messianic, multinational extension to the Jewish people.

As we set our minds to make the necessary changes, we may find it very difficult to admit that for centuries we were wrong scripturally—that we have strayed off course. It takes humility to admit error and courage to change false ideas that we have defended for so long. When researching historical backgrounds, cultural mores, idioms and word roots, we discover how far we have drifted from the truth. Looking up Hebrew and Greek definitions of such words as church, glory, holy, soul, etc. will give us a new approach to understanding the New Testament.

This is why it is imperative that we understand what God means when He refers to His people as His "chosen." To what have the offspring of Abraham, Isaac, and Jacob been chosen? They have been called and chosen to represent God, to introduce Him to the nations of the earth. They are called out to be different than the cultures around them. As believers in the Messiah, we are grafted into Israel as chosen people. We not only have access to the promises given to Israel, but we also have been given the same calling and responsibility to the world. The rites and trappings of Judaism are the vehicles God used to reveal to Israel His heart, motivations, and principles. All through the Old Testament, one can find passages[1] showing the preference of God toward following His principles and character over a strict adherence to rituals and rites.

· It is very important that we as Gentiles respect Jewish culture without trying to appropriate it for ourselves. We are grafted in, but still a distinct people group. We as Gentiles have the wonderful advantage of the richness of Jewish heritage and the freedom of Messiah. It is, therefore, our privilege to assimilate the character of our God and get about the task of our calling.

We therefore are not promoting the notion that born-again believers need to use Jewish traditions for worship such as a tallit, or follow Jewish practices, but rather, we encourage everyone to seek after a deep and full understanding of the issues of the heart of God. As we learn, we will find out that Jewish people may not be as blind as we have been taught to believe.[2]

---

[1] 1 Samuel 21:1–6; Luke 6:1–5 (David feeding the showbread to his men)
[2] Acts 15:17–19 (Counsel of Jerusalem)

CHAPTER TWELVE

Conclusion

Replacement Theology needs to be replaced!"
FRED WRIGHT

"The Lord is dropping a plumb line in the church.
It is frightening to see who is on the wrong side."
WENDY BECKETT

The purpose of this book is to warn about a rapidly expanding new movement in the Church that is subtly introducing the same old errors of the past. These errors eventually, but inevitably, led to centuries of atrocities against the Jews in the name of God.

An excerpt from the writings of Art Katz:

> From the Jewish Perspective, "Gentiles are to be despised and looked upon with contempt, as morally less than what Jews are, and historically, they have every reason to harbor this attitude. Through the ages, it has been the Gentiles who have inflicted suffering of every kind upon them, even in the name of Christ: the Crusaders with the white crosses on

their tunics, the Spanish Inquisition, the forced conversions under Catholicism, burnings at the stake, the expulsions, the pogroms, the Holocaust. It seems most Christians have no idea of how horrendous the Christian Church's relationship with the Jews has been through the ages."

There is nothing more repelling and more repugnant to the Jew than the name of Christ, because in that name they were historically persecuted, driven out, hunted down and burned at the stake. With that history of violence and bloodshed, however, it is still the Church whom God has chosen to be a blessing to the Jews and the nation of Israel.

Excerpts from Derek White of Christian Friends of Israel, UK:

> As the conflict in and around Israel continues and even worsens, there is the danger that an ever increasing number of Christians will turn against the clear, simple meaning of the Scripture concerning the return of the Jews to their land, and accept replacement theology. Not only will this cause the Church to abandon the Jews as a nation (Israel), but will, according to the plain teachings of the New Testament, expose her to the displeasure and judgment of God, resulting in unspeakable loss.

Has God abandoned His covenant with Israel because of her unfaithfulness, or for any other cause? Has He exchanged her with another body, the Church? If this was God's purpose, then He could, for the same reason, abandon the Church for similar reasons.

We had better look at the Church's history to understand that this is risky territory on which we tread. Throughout the past 1900 years up to the present day, the Church has had a depressing history. Our failures and our weaknesses are as numerous as those of Israel. Believers in Jesus Christ should be saddened because of the false doctrine, which has essentially led us into working against God, not for Him.

The predominately Gentile Church has received grace from God, and He requires us to show the same mercy to the Jewish people. We were once "strangers to the covenants of promise, having no hope and without God in the world" (Ephesians 2:11–13; Jeremiah 31:31–34). We, as Gentiles, have been brought into the New Covenant, which was originally established with Israel. This New Covenant still exists today and will never be altered, according to the promise of God.

For the past 19 centuries, the Church has totally failed to recognize that the Abrahamic covenant was an everlasting promise made by God Himself to the Jewish people. Instead, we selfishly and haughtily claimed all the promises made to the Jews solely as our own.

Subsequently, rejection and persecution of the Jewish people were launched. This may be our last chance to reconcile ourselves in these last days. God has given us the opportunity to show mercy, compassion and support for Israel before the final Day of Judgment arrives.

In this present day, there is a worldwide atmosphere of antagonism, terrorism, and total misunderstanding of Israel. There are many within the Church linking themselves with those who condemn Israel, misinterpreting their true roots in the Jewish olive tree. Replacement Theology and Islamic theology are in harmony against Israel, both refusing to recognize that Israel exists. God's covenant with Israel is everlasting and unconditional. If it were not for this covenant, Israel would not exist today. God is a covenant-keeping God and His promise for Israel will not be altered. Paul warned:

Be not arrogant towards the branches, but if you are arrogant, remember it is not you who supports the root, but the root supports you. . . . Do not be conceited but fear; for if God did not spare the natural branches, neither will He spare you. . . . Behold then the kindness and severity of God . . . to you, God's kindness, if you continue in His kindness; otherwise you also will be cut off. (Romans 11:13–22)

Chuck Cohen states,

Much of the Church has acted and still acts as though it has been grafted into a Christmas tree—flashing its attractive lights and decoration, but unconcerned about its roots and wondering why it is spiritually drying up and dying. As God pushes Israel toward her final destiny, world hostility, ignorance and self-righteous hypocrisy will grow ever more strongly even in the Church. It is not going to be easy to stand by the Word of God—but in the end it will be the only place worth standing.

Citing Malcolm Hedding once more:

The time is now for a mature Church to humble herself, recognize the in-grafting, thank God for His abundant mercy, and rise up to the measure of the blessing of Abraham. The Jewish people are still waiting for the full revelation of their Messiah, Jesus, Who is resident in His Jew-Gentile body, the Church.

Paul taught that true Gentile faith should make Israel jealous so that they would then find salvation in Messiah for themselves (Romans 11:11). As we have seen, the Church has generally failed to live up to this ideal, for reasons that lie in Church history, theology and practice.

Let us show the Jewish people a different attitude of unconditional love and compassion, the face of true Christianity that will reveal Jesus Christ, thus provoking them to jealousy. As you are seeing a need for the Church to recognize her mistakes, repent and begin to bless the Jews and the nation of Israel.

God wants to open up to His Church the mystery of Israel even as He prepares Israel to open up to the mystery of His gospel. Victor Schlatter in his book, *Where is the Body?*, mentions that,

> Scriptural reality reveals that there always has been and always will be only one unique family of Abraham. The Church will not be complete as the undivided Bride of Messiah until all the covenant promises to the Jewish people are ultimately fulfilled. Only then will all things close at the end of the ages as the Bible decrees!

Robert Stearns says,

> If we are truly concerned about preaching the gospel, we must repent for the demonically-inspired hatred that has, over the years, masqueraded as Christianity, and offer to others the healing and unconditional love that Jesus offers us.

As Israel is being more and more isolated and rejected by the nations of the world, we, as a growing remnant have a window of opportunity to bless Israel, pray and intercede for her, and be her friend during the difficult days ahead. I believe the harvest of the "lost sheep of the house of Israel" will come into the fold when the Church repents and takes her rightful role in welcoming her "elder brothers" into the family of the redeemed through their Messiah Jesus.

Paul's message in Romans 11:11 is a major key to world revival. As the Gentiles begin to fulfill their calling to provoke the "natural branches" to jealousy, large numbers of Jewish people will be grafted back into the Olive Tree. As Jew and Gentile worship the God of Israel as One New Man, it will mean nothing less than "life from the dead" — revival for all.

David Stern in his book, *Restoring the Jewishness of the Gospel*, writes:

> I believe that the reappearance of a Messianic Jewish community in our day is a significant phase of God's processes of saving all Israel. We Jews are beginning to recover our past. It is the task of Messianic Jews and of sympathetic Gentile Christians to work together to undo the damage caused by the division of the Jewish people and the Church.

As stated in the beginning of the book, the Gentile Christians are the "wild olive branches," therefore without the Hebrew perspective we are unable to have the same understanding as the "natural olive branches."

We live in a day of quick and unspeakable shakings. Our only way forward is to dwell fully in Christ, to embrace the insight that the holy Hebraic scriptures reveal and to move in the fullness of His Spirit.

The Jewish people have a prophetic role in the unfolding redemptive purposes of God in the earth. The Church needs to explore, learn, understand and appreciate the hundreds of scriptures relating to God's covenantal plans for Israel, His chosen people.

As we study the scriptures, may our hearts be attuned to the heart of God's love for His people and how we, the Church, fit into His plan for Israel's restoration.

The Church is at a critical crossroads. The day of neutrality is a thing of the past. In the words of Holocaust survivor Elie Wiesel,

The opposite of love is not hate, it is indifference . . . to remain silent and indifferent is the greatest sin of all . . . .

What would be the Church's stance if confronted with another potential Holocaust? Would history be repeated? Would another period of deafening and humiliating silence arise from the Church, or would a majority of God's people come to the aid of the Jews and the nation of Israel?

Closing Prayer

Father, we thank You for our spiritual roots. We thank You for the blessing that comes to us as an inheritance by being grafted into the Jewish olive tree.

Cleanse us from any remaining arrogance and ignorance that has caused such intense suffering for the Jewish people. Cleanse us from any self-serving theological bias. Cleanse us from incorrect interpretation of Your Holy Word. Father, reveal to us Your heart concerning your ancient people. Open our eyes so we can see how Israel fits into Your plans for the end of the age.

Lord, you have always had a faithful remnant in the Church that have understood the mystery of Israel. Lord thank you for stretching us spiritually and intellectually as we try to grasp the literal truths of Your word toward Israel.

We now recognize, in the light of scripture, Israel is a restored nation. The Jews are being regathered from the ends of the earth, and the natural and spiritual restoration has begun according to Ezekiel 36 – 37.

Lord, we now recognize that You have not forgotten or rejected Your ancient people. You are a faithful God who keeps His Covenant and You are again showing Your compassion to the Jewish people and the nation of Israel.

g Katly is

We commit ourselves to prayer for the restoration of the Jews back to their land. We pray that Jewish eyes will be opened to recognize their Messiah has come and will come again. We want to be a blessing to the Jewish people and the nation of Israel. We cannot change the past but we want to help change the present and engage for future involvement.

We want to acknowledge our indebtedness by standing with Israel in the midst of their present trials and to uphold Israel through faithful intercession. Help us to not be passive but proactive in seeking Your direction as we seek to give, serve and bless the Jewish people.

Lord, help us understand that Your return will be the climax of history for your Church and the culmination for Your people, Israel. In the light of scripture, the Church will not be complete until the "lost sheep of the house of Israel" are back in the fold. We anticipate a vast host of Messianic Jews welcoming You back with the words, "Blessed is He that comes in the name of the Lord!" We close our prayer with the words of Paul:

> Oh, the depth of the riches both of the wisdom and knowledge of God! How unsearchable are His judgments and His ways past finding out! For who has known the mind of the LORD? Or who has become His counselor? Or who has first given to Him and it shall be repaid to him? For of Him and through Him and to Him are all things, to whom be glory forever. Amen. (Romans 11:33–36)

Glossary

Allegorical Interpretation—Allegorical interpretation places on biblical literature a meaning that, with rare exceptions, it was never intended to convey.

Anti-Semitism and Anti-Zionism—hostility toward or discrimination against Jews as a religious, ethnic, or racial group.

Church Fathers—any of about 70 theologians in the period from the 2nd to the 7th century whose writing established and confirmed official church doctrine.

Crusades—any of the military expeditions undertaken by Christian powers in the 11th, 12th, and 13th centuries to win the Holy Land from the Muslims.

Deicide—the killing of God or a god.

Final Solution—"The Final Solution of the Jewish Question" also known as The Holocaust. An euphemistic name for both Nazi Germany's plan to completely annihilate all European Jews and their attempt to do so between 1941 and 1945.

Ghetto—a quarter of a city in which Jews were formerly required to live.

Hebraic mindset—A worldview seeking to read and understand the Bible from the Hebrew setting, culture and traditions in which it was written.

Hellenism—Word used to express the assimilation of Greek speech, manners, and culture, from the fourth century B.C. through the first century A.D.

Holocaust—The Holocaust was the systematic, bureaucratic, state-sponsored persecution and murder of approximately six million Jews by the Nazi regime and its collaborators. "Holocaust" is a word of Greek origin meaning "sacrifice by fire."

Inquisition—A Roman Catholic tribunal for discovery and punishment of heresy, which was marked by the severity of questioning and punishment and lack of rights afforded to the accused. While many people associate the Inquisition with Spain and Portugal, it was actually instituted by Pope Innocent III (1198–1216) in Rome.

Iron Cross—A military medal, the highest decoration for bravery awarded to the German armed forces in wartime. About 4.5 million were worn by the military. It was worn by all Nazis that carried out the Holocaust.

Literal Interpretation—Interpretation of scripture without allegorizing or spiritualizing, so that the sincere Bible student might resist conforming the Scriptures to any preconceived, theological conclusion; as well as ascertain what God Himself has desired to communicate to us in His written Word. An impossible goal apart from a consistent, literal interpretation of the Scriptures.

Pale of Settlement—Throughout Russia's history, the czars refused all Jews entry into Russia. The First Partition of Poland, in 1772, brought hundreds of thousands of Jews into Russian territory. Russia's rulers decided to restrict Jews to certain geographical areas, thereby creating the Pale of Settlement. The original Pale, established in 1791, included modern Poland, Ukraine, Lithuania and Belarus. Within the Pale itself, Jews were denied higher education and land ownership. The setting for the movie, *Fiddler on the Roof,* took place in Ukraine during the Pale, possibly in the late 1800's and early 1900's.

Platonism—A "school" of thought prominent in antiquity from the time of the founder Plato 428–348 B.C., up until at least the middle of the 6th century A.D. Platonism was unquestionably the dominant philosophical position in the ancient world over a period of more than 800 years.

Neo-Platonism—a philosophical system originated in Alexandria in the 3rd century A.D., founded on Platonic doctrine.

Pogrom—An organized, often officially encouraged massacre or persecution of a minority group, especially one conducted against Jews.

Replacement Theology: Another theological name is Supersessionism

- Israel (the Jewish people and the land) has been replaced by the Christian Church in the purposes of God, or, more precisely, the Church is the historic continuation of Israel to the exclusion of the former.

- The Jewish people are now no longer a "chosen people." In fact, they are no different from any other group, such as the English, Spanish, or Africans.

- Apart from repentance, the new birth, and incorporation into the Church, the Jewish people have no future, no hope, and no calling in the plan of God. The same is true for every other nation and group.

- Since Pentecost of Acts 2, the term "Israel," as found in the Bible, now refers to the Church.

- The promises, covenants and blessings ascribed to Israel in the Bible have been taken away from the Jews and given to the Church, which has superseded them. However, the Jews are subject to the curses found in the Bible, as a result of their rejection of Christ.

Righteous Gentiles — "Righteous Gentiles" is the phrase used for those non-Jews who risked their lives to save Jews during the Holocaust.

Zionism — Biblical Zionism is the firm belief that God chose the Jewish people and bequeathed to them as an everlasting possession the Land of Canaan, so that they should give to the world His Word, men of faith, the Messiah and a living example of what it means to follow this one true God and experience His faithfulness and correction. It holds that the modern restoration of Israel is not a political anomaly, but evidence of God's on-going faithfulness to His people through His covenant made with the Patriarch Abraham.

Bibliography

Beckett, Wendy D., *God Keeps Covenant—A Thirty-Day Study on God's Love for Israel*, Self Published, 2006

Booker, Dr. Richard, *How the Cross Became a Sword*, Sounds of the Trumpet Inc. 1994

Brown, Michael L., *Our hands Are Stained With Blood: The Tragic Story of the Church" and the Jewish People*. Gaithersburg, MD: Destiny Image Publishers, 1992

Cohen, Chuck and Karen *Homecoming: Our Return to Biblical Roots*, Sovereign world Ltd., P.O. Box 784 Ellel, Lancaster LA19DA, 2007

Diprose, Ronald E., *Israel and the Church: The Origin and Effects of Replacement Theology*, Authentic Media, 2004

Facius, Johannes, *Hastening the Coming of the Messiah*, Sovereign World Trust, P.O. Box 777, Tonbridge, Kent TN11 0ZS, UK

Finto, Don, *Your People Shall Be My People*, Regal, A Division of Gospel Light, Ventura, California, Copyright 2001

Flannery, Edward H., *The Anguish of the Jews*. The Macmillan Company, New York 1965

Garr, John D., Ph.D., *Restoring Our Lost legacy, Christianity's Hebrew Heritage*. Golden Key Books Restoration Foundation, P.O. Box 421218, Atlanta, GA 30342, 2001

Grubb, Norman, *Rees Howell's Intercessor*, Christian Literature Crusade, Fort Washington, PA 19034, 1980 Edition

Lindsay, Hal, *The Road to Holocaust,* Bantam Books, 666 Fifth Ave., NY 10103, Copyright 1989

Lutzer, Erwin W., *Hitler's Cross, The revealing Story of How the Cross of Christ Was Used as a Symbol of the Nazi Agenda,* Moody press, Chicago, 1995

Prince, Derek, *Prophetic Destinies, Who is Israel? Who is the Church?,* Creation House, Lake Mary, Florida, 1992

Scheller, Gustav, *Operation Exodus: Prophecy Being Fulfilled,* Ebenezer Emergency Fund International, Ebenezer House, 5a Poole Road, Bournemouth BH2 5QJ UK

Schlatter, Victor, *Where Is the Body?,* Destiny Image Publishers Inc. P.O. Box 310, Shippensburg, PA 17257, Copyright 1999

Stearns, Robert, *Prepare The Way (Or Get Out of the Way!),* Destiny Image, P.O. Box 310, Shippensburg, PA 17257-0310, 1999

Stern, David, *Restoring the Jewishness of the Gospel,* Messianic Jewish Resources International, 1988

Teplinsky, Sandra, *Why Care About Israel,* Chosen — A Division of Baker Publishing Group, P.O. Box 6287, Grand Rapids, MI 49516-6287

Wild Olive Website: Image in Chapter 4, Used by permission http://www.wildolive.co.uk/

Wilson, Dr. Marvin R., *Our Father Abraham: Jewish Roots of the Christian Faith.* Wm. B. Eerdmans Publishing Co., Grand Rapids/Cambridge

Wright, Fred., *Father Forgive Us. A Christian Response to the Church's Heritage of Jewish Persecution.* Olive Press, Monarch Books, Mill Hill, London, UK, 2002

About the Author

In 1948, as a twelve year old farm boy in southern Ohio, Merrill clearly heard the Lord saying, "You will be a voice in the wilderness, saying "Prepare the way of the Lord." For many years, this word was a mystery but over the past 63 years the call and vision has become clearer.

During the 1980's, Merrill Bolender and his wife Donna worked three years in Israel at Immanuel House in Jaffa/Tel Aviv.

During the Cold War, 1985–86, they went with a delegation from across the USA to the Soviet Union. They visited with Jewish families in Leningrad and Moscow that had applied to immigrate to Israel, but were refused and thus referred to as "refusniks." They, and other prayer groups at different times, interceded on Red Square for God to speak to Pharaoh, "Let My people go!" And, if necessary, visit plagues on the Soviet Union to bring her to her knees so the Jewish exodus could take place. After Chernobyl, drought, failed expansionist invasion in Afghanistan, the Cold War bankrupting the Soviet economy, a major earthquake in Armenia . . . the miracle happened. The Iron Curtain collapsed and the exodus began resulting in over a million Jews making their exodus to Israel.

Ebenezer Operation Exodus is an international ministry of intercessors with a prophetic calling of assisting Jews from the ends of the earth back to Israel in fulfillment of the prophets' predictions throughout scripture. Ebenezer Operation Exodus celebrated its twentieth anniversary in 2011, having begun in 1991 shortly after the fall of the Iron Curtain. The Bolenders served in Odessa, Ukraine in 2004 as intercessors for the Ebenezer Base. Odessa is a port on the Black Sea where ships sailed with Jewish passengers making Aliyah (immigration) to Israel.

Merrill and Donna have worked with Ebenezer Operation Exodus since 2004. They are presently Field Directors for the Western Great Lakes Region. Currently, they reside in a suburb of Indianapolis, Indiana. They come from ordinary backgrounds with an undeniable calling on their lives.